Spiritual Experience
The Revelation

By

Cid Antonio Leanos

FORWARD

Death, we come from, but we were unconscious, So we call it birth. We come from the unconscious, and we start to awaken as soon as we are born inside our mother; we become conscious, so we transfer and come from the unconscious to become conscious on earth, to know that experience we call awareness; in other words our I AM, and this is part of evolution that is completed at the time of consciousness. Everything else is icing on the cake. It might take longer to progress in the evolution without the matter experience. Still, progress is enableable, source is meant for growth in this life or after it, this was decided before your physical birth, so you don't have much to say in the matter because even your suffering is growth, especially suffering!.. You're just here to enjoy the ride by not creating mental problems out of situations, evolving past your ego, which is based on survival, and by releasing your gifts and emulating the divine. You can start to enjoy and release the heaven on earth that we all want and need.

It all begins as a feeling, which is your internal unconscious beliefs that will create your ideal world.

When this body "dies," the only difference is that we feel the transmutation of energy from one place to another, transitioning that scares us, but after, a new level of awareness sets in that gives you a sense of peace going into it, or for some after, even if they want to deny what's happened they have all eternity to discover their divine identity and come to terms with it.
We come from a source, and we go back to source, but now there is a new level of awareness of an individual expression of the same power which gave birth to itself by dividing itself, that is, you and I when we return to source and discover at the same time we are that same source. "I and the father are one" (John 10:30)
Answer me this!.. What isn't source?
Source is constantly manifesting itself in different levels of awareness that you cannot see beyond the awareness you perceive.

You must surrender your analytical mind to see beyond that is. Even while we live our lives, we are only 5% conscious and 95% unconscious. This means 95% of the time, you're not even aware of what's going on in your life or your body unless you're in harmony with the 95% percent by understanding. Until then, you will have the disorder, disease, or both as your constant companion.

Introduction

For those that read my previous book, this is a recap of my story from chapter 1 to chapter 6 that I highly recommend re-reading because when you repeat and remember you re-enforce the neuron patterns that support it.

In 2016 I started my journey, or should I say? I chose it to reveal itself to me before my 34th birthday, Disguised as pain and suffering that, in the end, would have cut short this experience called life. So to change this manifestation, I had to let go of my beliefs and habits(repetition of feeling that you practice and take action) that supported this ignorance that life conditions me to live. Now that I think about it, it was like a cleansing of my life's beliefs, perceptions, habits, and rituals by suffering to the point that my mind lost control of me.

Being present to execute these actions to deliver results takes practice and a lot of suffering, in my opinion, to surrender the illusion we were conditioned to believe only happence when there is no choice but to surrender. Don't get me wrong, I heard of people surrendering in a state of joy and bliss, but I personally haven't run into any that started that way; I keep on practicing and reinforcing the new rituals I have learned, and in this book, you will learn about them too and the feelings (unconscious beliefs) that help me enforce them....

The purpose of this book

Like Les Brown said "It's not to impress you but to impress upon you", that even if you don't have the skills and knowledge, you are more than capable of doing more. The extraordinary situation that you find yourself in at the moment is just a symptom of internal creation that has manifested. I honestly believe that you don't even know what you're capable of either, but if you think you do, you're not even close. This book will also show you that your brain and body act like, if not exactly like a machine that you have been privileged to have and that we are spirit, not body first or what science called it energy; that's how we control our physical world, "and by using the intellectual factor you can move an idea to manifest into form"- Bob Proctor.

"While the laws of the universe cannot be altered. They can be made to work under specific conditions, thereby producing results for individual advancement which cannot be obtained under the spontaneous working of the law provided by nature".

- Genevieve Behrend

The human brain and nervous system are engineered to react automatically and appropriately to the problems and challenges in the environment....

You act and feel: not according to what things are really like but according to the image your mind holds of what they are like.

-Maxwell Maltz

Table of Content

1 The situation

2 The decision

3 The Suffering

4 Insult to injury

5 The law of vibration & attraction

6. Ignorance is not bliss

7. Placebo

8. The human machine

9. Power

ONE

The Situation

I remember that day quite clearly, I was about to exercise in my living room when 'Doctor Oz'-the TV show started and this was the episode about how to think much more efficiently and this topic was pretty important to me at the time because I was currently having a lot of brain fog and feeling overly motivated (anxiety).

I thought that brain fog was happening to me because of aging and this was, I thought- "normal" for me. I wasn't taking into account all the caffeine drinks and energy powders that I was consuming at the same time during this situation.

So in the TV show, they mentioned 'Folic acid and how a person should take 800mg a day to have better brain function'. I just thought "It's just a vitamin and if I feel anything that I don't like I'll just stop taking it before anything happens". So I purchased the vitamins the next day and started to take them, as recommended by the TV show. Eventually, I took them for a whole month meanwhile still consuming the energy powders and other vitamins while waiting for a reaction.

I didn't know at the time that they had already included Folic acid in the "C4 Energy Powder"-I was already taking B-complex vitamins that I was adding to my daily routine. You know, I have a good idea of what you could possibly be imagining right now, but yes I was lacking awareness in this part of my life from which I learned a very hard lesson!

One morning, I woke up and felt very dizzy. I couldn't walk without throwing up. My head was spinning so fast that when I closed my eyes, It felt so much worse. I eventually went to the doctor and found out it was Vertigo. Meanwhile, I had Vertigo, and I couldn't eat nor take any of my supplements for a whole week which I deemed "a blessing in disguise", at the moment but it didn't last long. I was so happy that my vertigo had gone away but I was still in the dark about what the cause of it was. When I went to see the doctor, he couldn't explain why this was happening to me so I just took it as a coincidence. During this time, I did not know that my supplements with folic acid and C4 Energy powder were the cause of my ailments including vertigo.

I continued to take the folic acid with the b-complex and the energy powder after I got better from vertigo. So In my mind, I had made up a story that I couldn't do my job or function well without it.

My ego kept convincing me that it was just a one-time fluke and that it would never happen again. Basically, it was my condition that convinced me to keep taking the supplements and c4. The body and mind usually want to return to their conditioned state and with me as its slave instead of the master following.

In the following weeks, my health got better and I was taking my energy powder in low doses. At first, this was working for me but then my conditioned rituals came back and this time it was during a workout that my life made a drastic change.

I drank my pre-workout energy powder and I started to do my exercise not even 10 minutes went by before I remembered that my wife and I had plans to go to the movies.

So when we went to the movies, we got some popcorn and a soda like we always do but this time when I first took a sip of the soda, I felt that my heart started to go very fast and my blood pressure dropped. Because my hands started to feel sweaty, I started to get dizzy and my face was very pale with a blank stare, which made my wife notice that there was something wrong with me. But I didn't say anything because I didn't want her to worry.

I wanted her to enjoy the movie but my pride (ego) wouldn't let me admit that something was wrong. So I just sat there for 2 1/2 hours hoping that this feeling would pass but it didn't.

My left hand started to go numb then the left side of my cheek went numb including my jaw. I started to feel panicked but after the movie, I still went home instead of going to the hospital. When I got home, I walked back and forth In my living room thinking about what I should do while still feeling all my symptoms. At that moment, It was basically me versus my ego.

My body was telling me to go to the ER! But my mind was saying. 'Maybe this will pass'? I waited until 3:00 o'clock in the morning to go to the ER and exactly what I expected happened.

I walked into the lobby and signed in at the front desk. They gave me a number and took my blood pressure. My blood pressure 'I guess was stabilized by then' they told me I was OK, I told her I felt bad and that I took these supplements with soda that had caffeine. Even if the container clearly said not to take the energy powder with any more caffeine, "I thought my ego knew better", my ego's many years of experience with c4 thought it knew everything, but of course, it was wrong and I paid the prize.

So after 30 minutes in the lobby, they called me in. Set me in the hallway Till 5:00 o'clock in the morning, I saw a doctor pass by but didn't bother with me. By then my Symptoms started to go away. I got mad and just walk out and said to myself 'I'll see my own doctor the next day and I did exactly that but my doctor was booked up that day, so I went to the urgent care instead and I found out that urgent care is the same or if not more efficient than an ER, 'due to the low staff and lack of experience at lease in my case. In my urgent care appointment, I told the practitioner everything just like I did at the ER and basically, she just yelled at me because I have taken vitamins but didn't offer a solution but just her biased opinion that didn't help the situation. She told me I had an episode and that I was fine, but did not go too deeply into detail, just a basic overall exam.

I started to have heartburn, not to be cocky but I never had heartburn in my 34 years before this started, I was able to make an appointment with my doctor thinking it would be different somehow but somehow it wasn't because she came up with the conclusion it was only indigestion but for me, it didn't sound right because of what happened to me previously, but I listened to her because she is a doctor and at the time 'I used to believe that doctors knew everything and they are supposed to be right 100% of the time especially when they are playing with people's lives. My beliefs have changed quite a bit since then. I don't think of them like that anymore.

The doctor prescribed me milk of magnesium to my surprise it worked, later on, I found out that milk of magnesium is good for blood clots and healing to some degree of internal bleeding but too much of it can hurt your kidneys and can cause stomach ulcers.

After a couple of weeks, my "heartburn" went away and I remembered a very cool sensation crawling across my chest when I took the medicine. I'm pretty sure that, that type of sensation is supposed to come down to your stomach not across your chest as I felt.

Now after a month I started to feel a weird heartbeat behind my left shoulder blade and it used to move or should I say beat faster after moving or walking strenuously and my hands used to get numb and had full body tremors when exposed to any level of caffeine, I remember waking up at 4 am feeling the intensity of my whole body shaking and I walked to the living room sitting on the couch shaking when my cat came up to me in my time of need and just sat with me while this tremor past.

I knew I accidentally overdose on c4 and the supplements when I first took a sip of the soda in the theater that night, I literally felt a nerve in my head pop.

So I again made another appointment, I told her my new symptoms, she made a diagnosis and she came up that I had anxiety or some sort of depression. This kind of made me smirk a bit because if she knew my family background and issues, she would have known that I had suffered from depression since I was 7 years old, and now at 34, I have been passed that. I have gotten over it in my 20s or at least I Substituted with girls and alcohol. But I knew I didn't feel like I did when I was depressed and suicidal. This was something physically happening to me. 'I'm not saying you should party all the time to overcome depression because you can't run away or avoid the problem especially when they are in your own head'.

So the doctor gave me some (downers) medicine to calm my "anxiety" and told me to take half a pill when and if I had a tremor, later on, I started to have one and it didn't work.

Then made an appointment with a specialist about my tremors and numbness in my hands and all he did was poke me in one of my hands and said "Do you feel that?" I said yes but right now my hands are fine it comes and goes, I also asked him about the pop that occurred in my head at the time when all this started but there was no further acknowledgment, and wrote on my chart that I had depression followed by anxiety.

So even though I made appointments with different doctors to get their opinion, they read my chart and automatically ignored my cries for help.

TWO

THE DECISION
'Deciding not to decide is still a decision'.

Les Brown

The decision I decided to make was quite drastic but it was simple and made a lot of sense to me when I did it and it still does. It was that 'this is my life and nobody can save it for you, be what it is, but it's yours do something!' and by taking personal responsibility I was going to take my life back somehow. It was a form of surrendering the past. Only by focusing on the present moment what is here and now that I could change the imaginary future.

I started googling my symptoms, then I googled the natural cure for that symptom which led me to notice the physical part of my body that was harmed. I focused on a combination of vitamins, minerals, organic foods, plants, fruits, and vegetables. One of them was coq10 which is an antioxidant that your body produces naturally. Our cells use Coq10 for growth and maintenance. The level of Coq10 in our body decreases as we age. B-complex vitamins are needed by the body for energy production, synthesis of blood cells, healthy nervous system functions, and countless other metabolic processes. So I just want to clarify that the

B-complex wasn't helping me because of the combination I took with them, that was too much. Later, I started to search for higher quality that I needed and noticed made a big difference. So the coq10 is also good for the heart and makes the arteries more elastic in other words more flexible because the arteries harden over time due to unhealthy foods, diets, or medicines. Acetyl l-carnitine & Alpha-lipoic acid with Benfotiamine 150+alpha-lipoic acid 300, helped me rejuvenate my damaged nerves and helped dual radical-scavenging action to confront oxidative stress but please don't take more than needed because anything with excess can cause more harm than good. Do your own research and be your own advocate!

So my shoulder blade heartbeat started to diminish, my tremors started to stop and I could feel my hands again...hurray.

THREE

The Suffering

The acceptance of suffering is a journey into death. Facing deep pain allows it to be, taking your attention into It, is to enter death consciously. When you have died this death, you realize that there is no death — and there is nothing to fear. Only the ego dies.

-Eckart Tolle

I never really understood God before, I knew something was out there. But I didn't understand what it was. My religion really didn't help me at the time. It was kind of like a guide that was leading me in the wrong direction, but it was something instead of nothing. I thought that God would just be something that man made-up in order to understand life. Science made it obsolete so they decided to divide them. Well, that was my opinion...

When all this happened, I used to workout constantly because it used to balance my emotional life. So it's been a couple of months since I went to the gym and it's been a while in my opinion since my symptoms were not so frequent. I thought It would be a good time to start going to the gym again and for a while, I started feeling a bit confident and happy that everything was coming back to normal and I could have my life back.

So one night, I went to pick up my brother to go to the gym. He was motivated, and I was motivated. I thought 'What a perfect way to get started!' When we got to the gym he got on his treadmill next to me and I got on mine and just started walking and everything was good. I started to build up some sweat and after walking for about 15 to 20 minutes I decided to speed it up, not by much but enough to start Jogging.

This was one of those moments like they say "the calmness before the storm."

It was no coincidence that I unconsciously attracted my near death into my life. It was the most teachable moment and life-changing experience that started me down this path.

As I was running on the treadmill that night with my brother, I felt a sharp pain and then a tear that came across my chest. I instantly developed a cough and my breathing became shallow, my blood pressure dropped, and the heart monitor that the treadmill had instantly went up from 90, and it shot up to 160.

I gradually started slowing down. I didn't stop instantly because I was afraid of causing more damage, but bad news, the damage was done. There was no going back, my brother saw me and I could tell he was worried but did not react, just asking the occasional question. I'm trying to still pretend that nothing happened like everything was fine. I'm trying to do one more exercise machine but I couldn't and finally 15 minutes after just asked my brother that I wanted to go home and of course, he said ok. The drive to his house was very quiet and felt like a very long drive. I didn't know what I was going to do next. When I got to my house, I went past my wife and just went straight to bed. I was so scared I didn't know what to do and for some reason going to the ER was not my first reaction because of what had happened to me in my previous experience.

    I started praying like there was no tomorrow. I read all the scriptures that I remembered I had. I pleaded. I begged, after hours of praying, crying, and begging for a solution to this. I finally renounced myself to the situation. I remembered that I read somewhere that one of the symptoms when a person is going to have a heart attack they cannot sleep. So being 4:00 o'clock in the morning. I finally started to feel sleepy from all the fear and worrying. I remember telling myself to wake up in the morning, It felt like the right thing to do. Then the morning came and the first thing I said to myself 'I'm still here, I can feel my body still, I'm here, then I have a chance.' So I got out of one hole to fall into a deeper one!

The next day, I walked into an urgent care. I told them what happened to me and they did some tests. They used a monitor on my chest to see if I had a heart attack because they can only detect if your heart has been damaged but can't prevent it, everything came out good. They let me go, so the first doubt that came to mind was that the doctor can't detect it. Then why am I feeling this way, something doesn't add up either they don't know or I am smarter than them? I even was asking myself if I dreamed this. Was this real? I really tried to convince myself this was not true but for some strange reason, I felt a form of relief for like 20 minutes then my body couldn't maintain the thought and return to the experience it was exposed to. I still went to work! Thinking if I distract myself enough I could fix myself (denial). My reality started to set in quickly. I felt very thirsty during the day and started to develop a little bit of heartburn again but didn't really try to put too much attention to it but it persisted. It got stronger throughout the week and the heartburn got so strong that I stopped eating and drinking and developed a feeling that I was leaving and needed to prepare.

My mind started to justify me leaving, for example: for my wife, my mind was saying ... 'she will be fine, she will remarry' and then I started to think of my son, what will happen to him? because if my wife remarries how will they treat my son? especially knowing he's from a different marriage!

I remember how my childhood was very challenging for me, and I didn't want that for my son, growing up without a dad and never having a dad to look up to! always having questions about becoming a man. Especially during puberty growing up with shame and doubt about your body can be very depressing and frustrating. This frustration came from anger and disappointment, this disappointment was about me, my life, my situation, never doing anything good enough, being always afraid, scared, and in pain that was my constant companion.

I was thinking this was the end of my life and I have nothing to show for it but misery and suffering!

When I got home, I felt like I was in a trans and I remembered talking to my wife in the kitchen about something, then walking to the bathroom, and while I was looking in the mirror, my childhood started to flash on the screen of my mind like a movie, first, my teenager years, then young adult, and I didn't feel much about any of those experiences except disappointment! But when I got to the present I got angry, maybe even enraged! and I needed to do something about it but during this spiritual emotional moment there was a moment of clarity and a stillness that appeared, and in that stillness, a voice was able to breach through to this world that sounded exactly like my voice, if not exactly and said my name; it felt a sort of emptiness that followed and an intuitively feeling showed a picture of coq10 in my mind and without a doubt. I ran to my kitchen and grabbed the coq10 and swallowed 2 pills, instantly my heartburn was relieved and my thoughts subsided but my situation was far from over.

FOUR

INSULT TO INJURY

'A Doctor can either heal you or kill you depending on the level of belief you have in them'...

-Cid Leanos

Before my incident happened, I never really liked going to the doctor but I knew they knew something I didn't and the story my mind used to say was 'that I'll never be able to know as much as they know' so I caved into the hype that doctors know everything and medicine is good for you and can heal you, boy how wrong I was...

I decided to keep making doctor's appointments as long as I didn't take any of their prescriptions. I just used their technology that I didn't know how to personally use. When I used to go to an appointment, they always went through their standard procedures, and in my state of ignorance I used to tell them my symptoms then I used to tell them what I googled and that this could be the problem. They walked over to see my chart and automatically saw anxiety and their attitude towards me changed from being open-minded to assertive and aggressive this pattern kept on repeating with countless doctors except for one that was very kind and patient, also listened and responded to my needs. I think she was surprised by how many times I had been to the ER in such a few months, she was the reason I was able to keep my job and heal myself without a financial burden.

While I was in the process of healing myself, I was googling natural remedies for my symptoms but first I needed to know the cause and in order to find the cause, I went through countless blogs, and countless websites, and nitpick what made sense for me. There are a lot of opinions, and concepts that are misleading and you need to do this while being impersonal because when you're going through a health issue you are more emotionally involved in the topics and can easily create doubt, worry, and fear in you, it will scare you from doing what you need to do, but "when you burn the boats" like Tony Robbins says, being scared isn't an option.

I came across this natural remedy when one of my symptoms woke me up in the morning when I couldn't breathe and my chest felt heavy. I was panicking and quickly reacted by picking up my CBD vape pen that I bought at the time when I started to have tremors and instantly I was able to breathe about 50% better and of course, I went to the doctor's appointment and told them my symptoms, then they took x-rays looking for blood clots in my lungs but couldn't find anything. I later found out that only big blood clots are shown in X-rays and since mine were all small they went undetected. Only an MRI is able to see them but the doctor's excuse was "You're too young to have an MRI"...lol

I still don't know what exactly they meant when it's a life-or-death situation.

Later on that day, I was still in a panic, and for some reason, I thought again that the ER would take me more seriously than the doctor that saw me. So here I go walking into the ER at 1 am and again they took my x-rays and put me in a room with a machine that monitors my vitals. When the results came back they came back normal and they couldn't find out why my breathing was on and off on the monitors, even one of the male nurses told me to stop holding my breath and that's when my faith in the medical profession went out the window. What they ended up doing was that they gave me something to knock me out then woke me up at 6 am and gave some generic results that ended up giving me more anxiety.

So the natural remedy that I found was that sucking on a lemon or lime removes blood clots from your lungs.

That was the reason I had a strange cough that wouldn't go away.

A couple of weeks later I developed a stomach pain that settled on my lower left side and of course, I made another appointment just to hear an opinion, that's all. I knew I could find out what was the problem because now I could heal myself with my natural solutions. I found out that my spleen was enlarged by the doctor's appointment but the doctor couldn't explain why. But that was ok with me because of my new found confidence and healing remedies. I knew I could cure and heal my body.

I googled it and found that a spleen gets enlarged because of overuse. The spleen acts like a filter and it gets enlarged from working overtime. I was thinking, what is it filtering that is enlarging it? The blood gets filtered for blood clots and other things that I don't really know about, from the spleen enlargement I also developed some stomach bacteria that tested positive too, and was told if left untreated it could lead to stomach cancer. They tried to give me a prescription with antibiotics for the bacteria but I was reacting very badly to any medicine like heart attack symptoms bad, so I thanked the doctor but declined the medicine and walked out.

My internet search was the holistic doctor that gave me the options to pick from but I usually pick something that was close to my symptoms and went from there. Trial and error was my method. I know this was dangerous but I didn't have a choice. I wanted to live and I found a natural remedy for my stomach bacteria. It was garlic, lime, organic honey, and organic apple cider vinegar. I went back to the same doctor and took the same test and it came back negative. The doctor was surprised by my results and asked me what I did to heal this and I just answered with an 'I don't know!' and I didn't come back.

FIVE

The law of vibration & attraction

The Law of Vibration: states that everything in the universe is in a constant state of movement. We refer to these movements as vibration, and the speed or rate at which something vibrates is called its frequency.

The Law of Attraction: focuses on using your thoughts and feelings to dictate what you attract into your life. Attraction is a force acting mutually between particles of matter, tending to draw them together and resisting their separation.

-Proctor Gallager Institute

I need to apologize ahead of time because of my beliefs that I have concluded from my experience. I know that some of the audience I might offend by telling my true story and will criticize me because of my decision I made in this extreme situation but that was the best I could do at the time. I chooses to believe in something else regardless of the situation but I don't mean to hurt anyone or offend, I only wish the best to all who don't know that they are gods having a human experience.

I remembered close to my 20s my mom was watching a religious movie about Jesus Christ, the scene was when he was getting crucified, and I overheard my mom talking to my sister that he died when he was 34 years of age. My mind automatically made a conclusion this would happen to me at that age and I didn't doubt the idea even though the age was wrong. I didn't question it again from now on when I thought about it.

So when I was close to turning 34, I had a dream that I was getting chased by a large tiger and I got locked in a cage with the tiger, the animal started to bite and scratch me. But somehow in my dream I was able to defeat the tiger and I got out of the cage bloody and wounded but I survived. After that dream, I had one last surreal dream about a giant werewolf that was trying to knock the door down of a hotel I happen to find myself in. Before the dream ended I saw a big giant paw-like foot break through the bottom of the door then I woke up scared. This was very strange to me because I never had dreams like this before. I just ignored it. It was a lot easier for me, I didn't really believe much about stuff like that because I didn't understand it- NOW I understand that ignorance is not bliss, it actually creates and contributes to suffering!

By the time I got closer to 34, everything started to get momentum like a domino effect, and one by one started falling. One thing after another started to affect my health. The 4 sleepless months with tremors and numbness in my hands, were caused by nerve damage in my head. Then the heartburn was the side effect of the folic acid supplement with c4 energy powder that combined cauterize an artery to my shoulder blade that I tore while running on the treadmill causing internal bleeding.

I never understood why this was happening to me. I thought I was a good guy, I never picked on somebody, or stole from someone, in fact, they stole from me, I was the guy getting picked on, and then the question happened to pop up in my head. "Why do bad things happen to good people?"...I didn't know how to answer that question at the time! In my opinion, I had a challenging childhood with a hint of too much discipline, witnessed too much physical violence as a kid, and had no parental father figure, my mom was depressed and always got drunk to numb the pain of my father leaving us. Now, this! Come on!

Priming is when you are pre-conditioned to a circumstance before it happens for example when you see on the news that a new illness started to go around. We tend to "accept, believe, and surrender to the idea" as Dr. Joe Dispenza says. Then our brain starts to prime us for a circumstance to occur in order to be prepared when it happens. We are already setting an expectation which really means an intention. So it prepares you to expect something but in my interpretation, you also create it because they make you believe in illness. So when you encounter the so-called illness you already expect the worst-case scenario to be prime to encounter it. Proving your expectation even though the illness was never real but you happen to be the only one with it coincidence?

When you take into account The Observer Effect that on a quantum level, your presence affects the outcome of a situation.

In my life, I was already preconditioned or primed to expect a "bad" situation. I already had enough "bad experiences" which created the beliefs about the experience in order to reinforce my beliefs and kept attracting and expecting "bad experiences". When I started to expect a bad situation to happen to me It started to physically manifest in my body first by feeling like it already happened, then imagining how it happen and reacting like it was true, In the book Psycho-Cybernetics, Maxwell Maltz states that the body cannot distinguish between a thought and an actual experience and in this case, this is what we called fear being manifested in the body! That is usually called anxiety. When the idea is in harmony with the conditioning that I was exposed to on a continuous basis it can become automatic which is called a "habit" created directly from an unconscious or subconscious perspective.

Earl Nightingale explains that the mind is like a farm, and whatever you plant must return, the mind does not care what you plant but it must return what you planted- for example: if you plant corn you will get corn, and if you plant nightshade (a deadly poison) it will return equally in abundance as corn.

The mind is impersonal, it does not care what you plant and it will return what you plant.

From my experience and research, I had the pleasure to find out that God, the Universe, the Divine mind, and infinite intelligence work the same way as the mind, it is impersonal and it responds in a form of feelings and not to what you say or do, but what you feel in your heart to be true for you. The inner dialog is there to keep supporting that truth (belief) that your mind convinces you to be true (from an experience) and the thoughts you think are reinforcing it by creating how you usually feel on a day-by-day basis (subconscious).

Your subconscious/unconscious maintains the status quo feeling, meaning that the critical moments that you had in your life good, bad, or indifferent, and are holding in the psyche of your mind will start to dictate your primary feeling that you're constantly manifesting. It will constantly repel or attract a situation that only you have the power to change by changing your perception of the experience you believe you had, but it takes practice being present and a high level of awareness to not get pulled in by thought, feeling, emotion, situation by understanding that there is a higher good at play and surrender your beliefs that are no longer serving you anymore.

SIX

Ignorance is not bliss

ig·no·rance

1. lack of knowledge or information.

Definitions from Oxford Languages

When I created and attracted an experience that almost cut short this human experience and pushed me into a corner to find out what I really am, this was that moment that changed my life. When I found out that death is real for this body (which is your experience in this body) because we are always thinking it can happen to everyone except us. I found out personally firsthand that it's real and that after this, life is real too; when I found myself talking to myself, that was outside of myself and sounded exactly like myself without any conscious control and felt it was beyond my physical form, was the moment I knew I was close to leaving this body.

I went through a health situation that I ignorantly set an intention for unconsciously and was later surprised by it at the age of 34; I explained and found out that their different level of awareness/vibration/frequencies/consciousness/feelings and that they are so close to each other that there is no line to tell where one starts from and the other finishes. Every person is on a different level of awareness that dictates their level of understanding and it shows in the level of peace you have in your life; for example, Bob Proctor, in his seminar "You Were Born Rich," he explains that he can have a dog on the set and the dog wouldn't know, that he knows that he's a dog and it's on the set, the dog is aware of his outer world but not aware of his inner world, in other words, the dog is in a simple state of consciousness. We are in a self-conscious state, and we are able to see our objective(inner world) as well as are subjective(outer world). Some people are in a low conscious state/a low level of awareness; the awareness dictates how that person lives but knows a lot consciously but still in a low vibration(feeling, awareness, frequency) unconsciously; for example, they can have a masters or ph.D but still live in an animalistic state. They are not living there because they want to; they are living there because they are unaware of how to change it. They don't know that they don't know. Let that sink in for a minute!

The more you study, the more you develop understanding, understanding comes from knowledge, and it is the opposite of ignorance which means by understanding, you don't let the outside world dictate your goals and dreams because of your present or past results, hold the image regardless of your situation. We are always manifesting. You can't turn it off or on; the only difference why thoughts and things come into your life much faster than others is because of faith; faith is to believe in the invisible just; some people call it expectation or fear; fear is only possible when we are creating and expecting the things we don't want, we start to imagine it, and our body doesn't know the difference between an actual event or imaginary event and release a magnetic(thought) charge(feeling), so then you start to feel emotional which starts to attract, fear then starts to react chemically in the body creating anxiety. If you keep that emotion for an extended period of time, then it starts moving into disease, and after that, it moves into decay. To understand is the removal of ignorance which is key to living a healthy, wealthy, prosperous life.

A lot of people don't know how Reality really works, but that does not mean you will not get affected by it; the carnal mind(conscious mind) reacts to everything in your daily life, "it feels lack or limitation, and it impresses the subconscious mind" -Florence Scovel Shinn. As I said, and many others said it before me, 'Ignorant is not bliss.' Nothing is good nor bad. It just is, until we put our personal opinion from a precondition ideology that we carry about life, that you can always change when you understand the subconscious and conscious mind. I'm just saying that there's a good and a higher good, a higher good that we do not understand at that particular moment when things look like they're going wrong but later on, you'll find out that there was a higher agenda being executed beyond our understanding with your awakening in mind.

Here's an example, for instance: Take common sense. It's only common sense when you know something and the practice of that, and that you know now because it's important to you. Otherwise, it's not common sense. How can you help someone if they don't know they need help? Only when they know, then they will allow you to help them. This just shows you the different levels of awareness people have in different areas in their lives; for example, Price Pritchett, in his book YOU2 stated that "you have to forfeit some of your old beliefs and sacrifice some "sensible" thinking patterns," common sense is a self-imposed prison that put limits on you and your dreams so we must base our limits on uncommon sense because it's not common. "Rely too much on common sense, and you can expect to see common results."

- Price Prichett.

Mind is the Master power that molds and makes, And Man is Mind, and evermore he takes The tool of Thought and, shaping what he wills Brings forth a thousand joys, a thousand ills:-- He thinks in secret, and it comes to pass Environment is but his looking-glass.

-JAMES ALLEN

SEVEN

Placebo

pla·ce·bo ef·fect

1. a beneficial effect produced by a placebo drug or treatment, which cannot be attributed to the properties of the placebo itself, and must therefore be due to the patient's belief in that treatment

- Definitions from Oxford Languages

The placebo effect is basically, for me, just another form of hypnosis from an analytical point of view because you see matter in the form of a pill that your five senses are observing and concluding to be true for you. This conclusion is based from your five senses and agree to be true, you have all the supporting documents, and testimony, and of course, we have the Environment that keeps supporting our senses of the full body experience that are able to convince you that it is real to you. Therefore, your body makes it real once you have the supporting factors. You must give up conscious control for hypnosis to work, which is the placebo or nocebo of everyday life in the Environment you are in. The Environment is hypnotizing you.

In world war 2, Dr.Joe Dispenza wrote in his book you are the Placebo that a doctor by the name of Henry Beecher ran out of Anastasia and started using saline water as a substitute for morphine. I didn't believe that this actually happened and that this was administered to over 40% of soldiers and that they reported that the treatment eased their pain when undergoing surgery and treating wounds during this war. I googled this myself and was left without words that the actual body was reacting like a machine that can be influenced by a form of hypnosis to change our beliefs(conclusion and evolution) and can be convinced to accept things even if they are not true, especially when your Environment is supporting those beliefs like a doctor's office visit.

Does this sound familiar? In other words, what in your world do you keep perceiving to be true? And is this really helping you? Maybe it's time to re-evaluate certain parts of your beliefs that are not serving you anymore. Maybe in some part of your life, you had an experience that created a certain belief about that part of your life, and because of that, your life was created around that belief by either avoiding it or empowering it. Now you are only doing certain things in a certain way, and it starts to create havoc in your life if it's a disempowering belief.

This is also called a form of hypnosis when you accept something to be true with only assuming it to be true; as I stated before by Joe Dispenza, when you accept, believe, and surrender to a situation that you evaluated to be true by you or someone that convinces you, or even the Environment that influences you to think a certain way to make it true. This belief was implanted at a point in time that now you still carry in the psyche of your mind and don't even know it. In a study, Dr. Joe Dispenza went into detail about a famous example in a 1962 study in Japan with a group of children that were extremely allergic to poison ivy. The researcher rubbed one forearm of each child with a poison ivy leaf but told them that the leaf was harmless. As a control, they rubbed the child's other forearm with a harmless leaf that they claimed was poison ivy. All the children developed a rash on the arm rubbed with the harmless leaf that was thought to be poison ivy 11 of 13 children developed no rash at all where the poison had actually touched them. This was later called psychoneuroimmunology-the effect of thoughts and emotions on the immune system. Excepting, believing, and surrendering to manifest your conscious reality; as DR.Joe Dispenza stated, you need to surpass the analytical mind that controls the body that tells you how you perceive your environment, and that dictates time; those are the 3 things that he mention- the body, environment, and time.

I dedicated this chapter to Dr. Joe Dispenza (You Are The Placebo). I couldn't be more grateful to him and his research that helped me in my time of need to understand my analytical mind. It was this part of me that needed to know how things work to let myself experience Reality. Information to transformation was the key to starting my search for how Reality works and how I can start to enjoy my heaven on earth.

LET'S TALK ABOUT HYPNOSIS ...

So hypnosis It's just another way to say placebo without saying placebo, but it uses words and ideas that need to go in your subconscious by bypassing your conscious mind. Instead of pills or surgery to make you believe it is true, hypnosis is using words that cause you to release conscious control to alter your beliefs; otherwise, it wouldn't work. By you releasing control, you let someone or something have power over you, and now you are a slave to everything, and you are reacting instead of responding, and ironically it is the same way to rewrite it too, but with your goal in mind because you are programming you not the other way around, we are always getting program, but this time you are in the driver seat and not the passenger. For example, when a hypnotist has guided you to the point where they are convinced that the hypnotist's words are true statements and also does a simple trick to re-enforce the experience by telling you to look up and then telling you to try to open your eyes but you can't, then you automatically assume that they have you under control which enforces the experience. The person then acts differently because he thinks and believes differently. Remember this, it doesn't matter where you got the idea from or where you picked it up; it only matters if you firmly conclude that the idea is true. This would have the same results as a hypnotist hypnotizing you. So the hypnotists can only hypnotize you if you believe the words are true or what you imagine to be true for you, and the people on the stage that are acting differently from who they are, is because they let themselves be hypnotized, they let themselves be convinced; they were open to accepting a new idea to be implanted in the subconscious mind which change their attitude(their action, thoughts, and feelings). The funny thing about this is that you don't need to go anywhere to get hypnotized; this is happening on a daily basis right underneath your conscious control because most of our lives are on autopilot, meaning you are not even aware of what's going on, in a way you are already hypnotized and the programs in your subconscious are running by themselves which is the autopilot, you might as well hypnotize yourself consciously and implant your goals &

dreams that you want and deserve because if you don't, someone will do it for you and I guaranteed you're not gonna like it. If you're not living the life of your dreams, then you better start noticing the programs by starting to dehypnotize yourself from false beliefs by really acknowledging the actions that you're doing without your awareness. Meditation is a great tool to dehypnotize yourself by getting control of the autonomic nervous system (a component of the peripheral nervous system that regulates involuntary physiologic processes including heart rate, blood pressure, respiration, digestion, and sexual arousal), which is the seat of your subconscious in the body, by relaxing the system and overwriting the precondition factors. Meditation will help you notice the ideas that don't serve you anymore, and really consciously notice them and let them go, then ask yourself, does this action, idea, or belief makes sense for my goals? Or am I living on purpose ?. In other words, being clear on what you want will help you achieve your goals. Maxwell Maltz, in his book Psycho-Cybernetics, explains: that there is an abundance of scientific evidence that shows that the human brain and nervous system operates purposefully in accordance with the know principles of cybernetics to accomplish goal of the individual. In so far as function is concerned, the brain and nervous system constitute a marvelous and complex "goal-striving mechanism," a sort of built-in automatic guidance system that works for you as a "success mechanism" or against you as a "failure mechanism" depending on how "YOU," the operator, operate it and the goals you set for it.

EIGHT

The Human Machine

The self-image is changed, for better or worse not by intellect alone, or by intellectual knowledge alone, but by "experience." Wittingly or unwittingly you developed your self-image by your creative experiencing in the past. You can change it by the same method. It is not the child who is taught about love but the child who has experience love that grows into a healthy, happy, well-adjusted adjusted adult.

-Maxwell Maltz

Like Maxwell Maltz stated that we are the operator of this body (organic machine). The operator and the body are compared to a computer that we can control and operate, but sometimes we jam it by giving too many problems to solve at once. The computer can do all the work for you, but it's the responsibility of the operator to set the goal. We set our goals through our beliefs, expectation, ideas, perceptions, and many other things that influence us in our daily life, and we try to solve them by conscious control, trying to use are forebrain in a way it wasn't designed to be used. If the operator goes through an experience that creates suffering and is impressed on the subconscious mind (successful mechanism), then your successful mechanism turns into a failure mechanism because the brain (the survival machine) is built to survive in this world by putting danger first for you to notice in order to be aware of them. If you let your mind impress danger in your subconscious, then your mind will torture you to protect you like a double edge sword. This creates anxiety and suffering on many levels that you are not aware of. Understanding that you are spirit first that has a body, "that has been gifted with an intellect, and by learning to use this intellectual factor that can manipulate matter that moves this body into form" (results) -Bob Proctor. The carnal mind/conscious mind was never meant to create but only to direct, and that's when you get into trouble by trying to take everything on by will alone, thinking that you know more than infinity intelligence which is at the same time your subconscious mind that does all the work for you every day without your conscious awareness like heal your cuts, bruises, digest your food, builds your muscles, keep your body temperature regulation and many other things that we take for granted in our daily life like James Allen said: "we wait as one that understands when spirit raises and commands god is ready to obey." It's been said that by practicing, you can create a habit, but a habit is a feeling, not necessarily an action but the practice of the feeling and moving into action that keeps the habit in place. For example, walking it's a habit we created since birth but keep on being re-enforced every time we walk, but if we stop practicing that habit feeling to walk, we stop utilizing it, and our leg muscles will start getting weaker to the point we can't walk anymore, and muscles memory goes out the window, and now we need to regrow a new set of nerve connection to relearn and stimulate our muscles to act. So a habit is not set in stone and can be changed, altered, improved, or removed by being consciously aware of it by not acting on the feeling or urge to satisfy a habit, and the brain can also create habits of its own if not monetized by you for example when you know a doughnut is bad for you but have the habit or feeling to satisfy that urge or craving because your body and brain know the chemical high (stimulation) it will get from the sugar that will create pleasure. Maybe I'm going a bit overboard on the example of walking, but the point that I am trying to get across is that a habit is a feeling that turns into an action that we practice, so habits are really feelings that you habitually have that can also be considered a ritual in other words (something that you do or often feel that can be triggered by Environment or a thought that will make you move into action in a physical or nonphysical manner), ignoring the feelings by understanding helps you to have conscious control to change the habit. The body becoming the mind or the mind in the body, both play a significant role in how you think and feel about what you're doing but only being aware will help you to make a conscious choice; only then you'll be free from what is called bondage, if not you will follow your predetermined destiny that some people call fate. We all react to our mind, which is constantly telling us what we believe is happening to us; there is no clear picture with the filters of life experience and the conclusions we made from those experiences; this is always affecting how we are reacting to situations that appear in our life. Just like a machine programmed to be and react to what the programmer programmed. We are that programmer, and we also have programs from past programmers like your mom and dad, grandparents, or great-grandparents that passed down their biological evolution in our DNA; that's why you look the way you look or are more prone to react or act to situations in certain ways than others, for me I'm very analytical that means that for me to understand something their have to be useful information supporting the idea to make a solid evolution, otherwise it doesn't make sense to me "I need to connect the dots" In spirituality theirs a practice to manifest your vision and it requires to trust the process and the analytical part of me always try to interfere with my practice, so I go back to the foundation that helps me understand and that is quantum physics explaining (THE OBSERVER EFFECT) Quantum Theory Demonstrated: Observation affects Reality that tells us that by the act of watching, the observer affects the observed Reality. Weizmann Institute of Science, February 27, 1998. So thought of you expecting something creates something, and by reminding myself that it's been proven time and time again, gives my analytical mind peace of mind and doesn't affect me when I fail to manifest something in my life; it gives me patience because I know it is possible. Just like learning how to drive, we don't really know what to do, but we have a good idea of how to do it. It is the experience that re-enforces our knowledge, and as a result, we get confident because we know that we know and nobody can tell us otherwise until we start learning something new in the same category. Then we become the student again, but you are on a higher level from where we started; that kinda sounds like life in a nutshell.

NINE

POWER

Law of conservation of energy:

The first law of thermodynamics simply states that energy can : neither be created nor destroyed it is the conservation of energy

Dec 6, 2014

Triggers create a form of power that can strike us like a burning desire out of nowhere and can destroy us when theirs is no direction or clear understanding, and understanding can lead us to master this energy being released from you because it comes in a blink of an eye, you have the power of ten men, or the motivation to climb all obstacles in your way or get through whatever you need to get through with such energy that you don't believe it yourself. Such great created power must be directed, and it is only by understanding that you can use your triggers by consciously programming them to serve you; for example, I implanted a trigger that every time I feel that I have no conscious control over a situation or a thought, I let go of everything that I can't mentally or physically control, and by letting go I mean surrendering the situation to a higher power that resides in us. I can let the success mechanism work for me by getting out of the way. If you're not aware of your triggers and you don't learn to control them, then your ego will control them for you by implanting all its ideas that it experiences and only find ways to work from envy, jealousy, hate, greed, and all the other emotions that create suffering because everyone is better than you and you don't have what you want from the ego's point of view. This can trigger anger being used by ego (evil) and then either directed at the person or directed at you, the host. The ego is a survival mechanism; we have to survive on this planet more like an animal surviving in the wild, and it will use anything it can to get its way in order to live the way it wants to by force. You must understand that you are not your body or your brain, but we live in a body, and we have a brain that can use us; if we are not aware of who we are beyond body and mind as Eckhart Tolle said, I am not my thoughts, emotions, sense perceptions and experience. I am not the content of my life. I am life. I Am the space in which all things happen. I am consciousness. I am the Now. I AM. This can have dire consequences for letting the survival mechanism(ego) run the show. Start by questioning every Thought that creates fear or anger in your body. Ask questions to yourself, Does this Thought makes sense to me?... Would I want this in my life? .. Do I want this to happen to me or something better?.. One trick that works for me is to analyze the Thought consciously and whatever comes to light becomes the light. In other words, don't just let any thought pass without your conscious awareness of it; think about it like a garden, and you must attend to it; otherwise, the weeds will take over. Triggers are basically emotional reactions that have been conditioned by repetition to the body and influence the mind by responding automatically without your conscious control; all this happens after you made a conclusion about a situation and evaluate that this is the best way to react accordingly to the level of awareness you hold at the time. This doesn't mean it is good or bad; it just means that you act the best you knew how; that's all until you notice that that way isn't serving you anymore, that you need to re-evaluate that reaction because it's not accurate to what is happening at that particular moment. You need to redefine yourself about what is happening NOW.

If you don't get what you manifest at the time instantaneously in front of your eyes or at will, is because you haven't convinced yourself that you have it yet !.. your body and the mind are not in harmony for that manifestation to occur; it is some sort of doubt! You need to feel it into existence to manifest your creation. So now you need to move into action to satisfy your analytical part of your brain to believe it's possible that you will have it; in other words, you need to convince and train your ego/brain to look for the reasons to let your analytical part except, to make it possible and it's through knowledge and the understanding of that knowledge of you that will make this possible because we don't get what we want, but we get what we are.

In conclusion .....

My life has changed like night and day and I can never go back to who I was before this incident, nor would I. What I learned is that ignorance is not bliss, it is suffering, it is misery, it is pain and poverty.

So basically I attracted my own death at one point in my life because I was ignorant of the laws of the universe, and ignorance is no excuse because we all reap what we sow consciously or unconsciously and my dad was a victim of his own mind, he didn't know that there was a choice but now you do. The law is impersonal, it has no opinion of what you're planting, you could be young, you could be old, male, female but guaranteed you're going to get it back.

So why not feel worthy of riches, health, love, joy, and peace? It all starts by controlling your thoughts, and feelings and being aware of your beliefs, taking personal responsibility for what you planted in your farm and not reacting to your emotional reactions by controlling the inner dialog that maintains your emotions which are your subconscious thoughts ...

GOALS- **learning objective BONUS**

1. Staying calm while still Healing.
Consciously choose the reason, why you want to heal yourself. (find a deep meaning)

HomeWork: write down a list of all the things you care about, This can include anything. (breath don't think and feel the truth) Then pick your priorities, Then write a phrase that can help summarize everything important to you. (this is your meaning, you'll feel it to be true)

2. Looking for solutions, not problems.
Go into action regardless of the situation.

Use a mantra that will give you peace until you find your solution.

I use Google to search for solutions to heal myself since the medical field had given up on me I had to find a way. (it's my life anyway, why are they responsible for it!)

Once you diagnose your health problems then start to find an organic solution.

Use the most organic medicine which can be vitamins, minerals, herbs, and a combination or mixture of medical technology. Keep your doctor's appointment and listen for clues. Then go searching for solutions if need be. It may feel like trying to find a needle in a haystack but keep at it! You're not alone! I DID IT! So you can too!...When you are tired or frustrated that means your doing this right. Find a way or make a way!
(I'am not saying to break the law but all bets are off now!.. We are talking about a permanent health solution, Not a band-aid, So please don't hurt anybody)

3. Maintaining your patience is based on faith & understanding.

After you found the right combination of organic holistic remedies, supplements, rituals, treatments, eating habits, sleeping habits, drinking habits, talking habits, feeling habits, we all make mistake, I know I did because I had to learn something new, Don't stop until you get your results that you want!.... Even then don't stop keep healing, keep improving stay with the momentum. Now that your physical health is much better.

Once you and your brain notice the slow but improving results, you will get momentum and some degree of negative talk will subside and faith with courage will take its place.

(**HomeWork**: Read DR. Joe Dispenza- YOU ARE THE PLACEBO)

4. Persistence is key!

See your plan, and feel it into reality. Our body does not know the difference between a thought and a physical situation that's how hypnosis works.

Never settle for second place especially when second place means death!.. We are talking about your health, right? We are NOT talking about a game. This is serious! the clock has started, it's about time you see it! The situation you find yourself in is strategically designed for you to overcome. The battle was always an illusion. This suffering was made to make you better, the mental block, the environment, the doctors, your parents, your friends, your siblings whatever you feel and see as a PROBLEM... love has always been the prime objective.

THANK YOU!

I would like to Thank you for reading and being a part of my life, and I pray that my found Knowledge in this book helps you in more ways than one, so that you may have the strength to help others with much love and joy may you find light where there is dark, and replace suffering for peace by discovering who you are in this never-ending story call life. So be it, it is done!

Edited By

Cid Antonio Leanos

DEDICATION

Giovanni Delcid Leanos

Giulianni Josue Leanos

Itzel Gianni Leanos

Raquel Leanos

For questions or Interviews

www.instagram.com/cidleanos/

Facebook.com/Cid leanos

Cid_leanos@yahoo.com

www.ingramcontent.com/pod-product-compliance
Lightning Source LLC
LaVergne TN
LVHW031607060526
838201LV00063B/4759